GENERATION IDENTITY

Original: *Die identitäre Generation*, London: Arktos, 2013.

First English edition published in 2013 by Arktos Media Ltd.

Copyright © 2013 by Arktos Media Ltd.

Published in the United Kingdom.

ISBN **978-1-907166-41-9**

BIC classification:
Social & political philosophy (HPS)
Nationalism (JPFN)

Translation: David Schreiber
Editor: John B. Morgan
Cover Design: Andreas Nilsson
Layout: Daniel Friberg

ARKTOS MEDIA LTD
w w w . a r k t o s . c o m

Markus Willinger

GENERATION IDENTITY

A DECLARATION OF WAR AGAINST THE '68ERS

ARKTOS
London, 2013

TABLE OF CONTENTS

FOREWORD: THE FRONT LINE
by Philippe Vardon

'Because we are old enough to face all challenges
and have an enormous responsibility towards
history, we have made the choice to resist.'
– Manifeste des Jeunesses Identitaires
(Manifesto of Identitarian Youth), September 2002

'People try to put us down — Talkin' 'bout my generation
Just because we get around — Talkin' 'bout my generation'
– The Who, 'My Generation'

Abandoned, isolated, atomised, uprooted. Without memory...and thus without a compass for the future — this is how they wanted us. More approachable for the merchants, more gullible for the media, more docile for the rulers. But something went wrong with the plan, as the present work shows.

Generation identity is first of all the generation which one would rightly have imagined to be without identity. One supposed it to be purely hedonistic, profit-oriented, individualistic and concerned with the question 'What shall I do?' (with MY life, MY money, for MY career). Instead it has astonished the whole world by proving itself to be far more profound, with each person addressing the question 'Who am I?' first, and then 'Who are we?' Our leaders, who have spent their entire lives in pursuit of enjoyment (and

7

who continue to do so all the more), hardly expected that some dissidents would spring up from within this generation to choose being over mere appearance, and being over having. Perhaps we have found evidence of the famous millennium bug, since this is a real error in their software...

They imposed unchecked mass immigration throughout Europe in order to push their march towards triumphant multiculturalism and a global village. What a huge mistake! While the economic, social, cultural and security consequences of this immigration are no doubt terrible, like the zealous quislings of this flood, I too shall shout out loud and clear that 'immigration is an opportunity!' Am I being provocative? Sure, but I see immigration as an opportunity because it has enabled the reawakening of our people—of our peoples. For it is in the face of the Other that the notion of 'we' acquires meaning. It is in the face of the Persians that the Spartans and Athenians discovered themselves as Greeks. Likewise, it is through the confrontation of young Frenchmen with extra-European immigration, and hence their new awareness of mutual differences, that the identitarian dream has emerged. This (often difficult, sometimes violent) dream has turned into a resistance movement, and shall tomorrow turn into a Reconquest.

They have defiled our flags, erased our frontiers, twisted the very names of things. With them, the homeland is no longer the land of one's fathers! It turns into a nebulous idea, an abstraction, a construct. For us it represents the most concrete things of all: our words and songs, our forests and mountains, our bell-towers and castles, our relatives' graves and our babies' cradles. We carry our flag within us and trace our frontiers ourselves: this is our identity! The agents of the system for killing peoples—to quote Guillaume Faye's formidable formula—would like to break the chain of our heritage: we're here to fix its links.

The identitarian struggle—which certainly promotes an ideal and certainly revolves around specific ideas—is far more than simply an 'ideological' matter. It is a struggle for continuity (since identity is not the past, but rather that which never passes on), or to put it more clearly: survival. It a struggle which we cannot flee from or reject without losing our dignity as upright men.

Markus Willinger's declaration of war no doubt presents some personal considerations — since acting as the spokesperson for a group does not mean losing one's unique voice — and hence some minor points the reader (just like the present writer) might disagree with. Still, this work sums up many of the ideas and concepts of the identitarian struggle that began (in this form) in France in 2002 and which now finds echoes across many sister-countries. This text, therefore, falls directly within the sphere of the challenge launched by the youngest identitarian militants (through the movement Génération Identitaire, founded in August 2012 and made widely known by the — symbolic — occupation of the mosque in Poitiers) against the generation of the '68ers, who hold prominent posts of responsibility in almost all sectors of society and who are largely responsible for the chaos we must currently face.

I shall bring this Foreword to a conclusion by inviting all readers to support an idea that we have always sought to keep alive in our way of envisaging the political-cultural struggle we are waging and which — I believe — determines a number of reactions and attitudes. Some people, steeped in a form of morbid romanticism (which may have its charm in the musical or literary sphere but which proves disastrous in the sphere of political activism), complacently mope about in their self-appointed role as the 'last men standing.' They perceive themselves as the rear guard of a dying world, and see their fight as all the more beautiful because it is clearly destined to be lost. This attitude is both comforting (for if the struggle is already lost, there is no point in making any inevitably vain efforts) and completely suicidal.

On the contrary, the identitarians are the avant-garde, or better still the front line! Far from being the last expression of a world in its death throes, they are the first pangs of a new birth (according to the very etymology of the word 'revolution'). To use a different image, the identitarians are not those who are watching a dying flame, but rather are a thousand torches which light up in the night.

Reach out your hands too, my friend, grab the torch and set it alight!

(Translated by Sergio Knipe)

Philippe Vardon (b. 1980) holds a degree in Political Science. In 2002, he was one of the founders of the identitarian movement in France, starting with its youth movement, Jeunesses Identitaires, and he also assisted in the creation of Bloc Identitaire, the primary identitarian organisation in France today. He was the chief spokesman of Jeunesses Identitaires for five years. In 2007, he formed a local branch of the identitarian movement in his hometown of Nice called Nissa Rebela which has participated in the local elections. He ran for mayor of Nice in 2008, and in subsequent elections he has run for other positions. Additionally, he now leads Les Identitaires, the think-tank of the French identitarian movement.

EDITOR'S NOTE

This book makes frequent use of the term '68ers, which is a common term in Western Europe but not in the English-speaking world. It refers to the generation that came of age around 1968, and which was responsible for many of the Marxist-inspired political and social upheavals which took place at the time, most particularly the massive strikes in France during that year. A group of students and sympathisers occupied the administration building at Paris X Nanterre University in March of that year in order to protest what they perceived as class discrimination in French society, causing the university's administration to call in the police to end it. Protests continued there for the next two months, and by May, they grew to encompass many other schools and groups, bringing about the largest general strike in history and effectively shutting down the country, nearly causing the collapse of the government. While similar protests took place throughout many nations at the time, the French strike was by far the largest and most effective. Although the 1968 protests were unsuccessful in achieving their goal of instigating a revolution, they nevertheless marked the beginning of an age of liberal political reforms in those nations. These reforms, and their consequences, have continued to dominate the political and cultural landscape of Western Europe ever since, and have been termed the 'new social movements.' Many of the student demonstrators of 1968 went on to assume prominent roles in politics, academia and culture in subsequent years, and were able to use their positions of authority to further inculcate the ideals of their youthful radicalism into the mainstream. '68ers is therefore similar to the term 'baby boomer' that is used in the United States to refer to those Americans born in the generation after the Second World War, many of whom became hippies, anti-war activists and other would-be revolutionaries during the 1960s, and some of whom went on to become crusaders for liberal causes in their later careers.

This book, as is obvious from the title, also makes frequent use of the terms 'identity' and 'identitarian.' The French 'New Right' author Guillaume Faye, in his book *Why We Fight: Manifesto of the European Resistance*, has defined identity in this way: 'A people's identity is what makes it incomparable and irreplaceable.' He goes on to elaborate:

> Characteristic of humanity is the diversity and singularity of its many peoples and cultures. Every form of its homogenisation is synonymous with death, as well as with sclerosis and entropy. Universalism always seeks to marginalise identity in the name of a single, unique anthropological model. But ethnic and cultural identities form a bloc: maintaining and developing the cultural heritage presupposes a people's ethnic commonality. [...] Look: identity's basis is biological; without it, the realms of culture and civilisation are unsustainable. Said differently: a people's identity, memory, and projects come from a specific hereditary disposition. [...] Identity is never fixed or frozen. It remains itself in changing, reconciling being and becoming. Identity is dynamic, never static or purely conservative. Identity should be seen as the foundation of a movement that endures through history — the generational continuity of a people. Dialectical notions associating identity and continuity permits a people to be the producer of its own history. (From *Why We Fight* [London: Arktos, 2011], pp. 171-173)

Those individuals and groups which have been inspired by this concept of identity throughout Europe are frequently referred to as 'identitarians.'

–John B. Morgan, 5 April 2013

PREFACE

Europe is in a deep crisis. This crisis weighs more heavily than the division of Europe by the Iron Curtain, or the destruction of our continent during both world wars.

This crisis is fundamentally different from others that we have lived through. It is a crisis of the European spirit.

After the National Socialist reign of terror, our continent fell sick and lost its will to live.

The next generation, the '68ers, hated and condemned everything that had been passed down to them: every tradition, every belief in their own kind, every will toward an authentic identity.

This belief that one's own kind is worthless—that cultures, peoples, and families count for nothing and need to be rooted out—threatens to end Europe's existence as a continent for Europeans.

The people of Europe have lost their will to live; they are dying out, because they don't want to thrive any longer, because they don't want to have any more children, and because they've forgotten what it means to stand up and fight for one's own.

The ideology of the '68ers has infected Europe. It is a sickness that will kill us if we don't find a cure. Even if we've lost our will to power, our neighbours haven't, and they're already penetrating our borders and occupying the places that we freely surrender to them.

The ideology of the '68ers is divorced from reality and cannot endure in the long run. It will pass with time. Either we Europeans will recover and free ourselves from it, or it will drag Europe into the abyss, and we will both disappear together.

*

Never before in human history have foreign peoples invaded to such an extent into a populated region without encountering any resistance from its indigenous residents. That Europe is coming to an end after thousands of years of a proud history is not due to the strength of the invaders, but rather to our unwillingness to fight for our own survival.

The '68ers have made affirming our own identity into something bad. They've associated it with war, destruction, mass murder and violence.

They've made us so doubtful of our own self-worth that we don't dare to defend ourselves; we silently endure whatever others do to us.

We're so afraid of being labelled 'racists' that we unconditionally accept anti-European racism.

When the '68ers took power in Europe, they didn't just allow the mass immigration of foreign peoples into Europe; they actively promoted this development. They called it multiculturalism.

We young Europeans grew up on a continent that doesn't belong to us anymore. We have only known a culture in collapse, our peoples at the ends of their lives. We had to withstand the attempts of our parents and grandparents to uproot us and make us into 'individuals' without any identity. They want us to rejoice that Europe is falling, to accept and submit to its defeat. But we won't. We rebel.

*

A new political current is sweeping through Europe. It has one goal, one symbol, and one thought: Identity.

It is the current of our generation. It represents European youth. A youth that wants the one thing that the ideology of the '68ers can't give it: a future.

Emanating from France, that proud and noble land, this new current is sweeping countless Europeans along with it. It is taking form and proclaiming the end of the era of the '68ers, a new epoch, the age of a new generation: generation identity.

Our generation is rising up to dethrone the '68ers. This book is no simple manifesto. It is a declaration of war. A declaration of war against everything that makes Europe sick and drives it to ruin, against the false ideology of the '68ers. This is us declaring war on you.

1.

GENERATION IDENTITY

You want to know who we are? Where we come from? What moves us?

We'll tell you.

We are the changing times; we are the rising wind; the new generation. We are the answer to you, for we are your children.

You've thrown us into this world, uprooted and disoriented, without telling us where to go, or where our path lies. You've destroyed every means for us to orient ourselves.

You've reduced the Church to rubble, so that now only a few of us still find refuge in the ruins of that community.

You've devalued the state, so that none of us wants to serve it anymore.

You've split the family. Our domestic idyll has been plunged into divorce, conflict and violence.

You've subjected love to a reductionist deconstruction, and so instead of a deep bond, only the animal drive remains.

You've ruined the economy, so we inherit mountains of debt.

You've questioned and criticised everything, so we now believe in nothing and no one.

You've left us no values, yet you now accuse us of being amoral.

But we are not.

*

You've promised yourselves a utopia, a peaceful, multicultural society of prosperity and tolerance.

We are the heirs of this utopia, and our reality looks very different.

You buy your peace with ever-mounting debt.

Today, we're watching your prosperity disappear throughout Europe.

For us, your multicultural society means nothing but hatred and violence.

In the name of your 'tolerance' you hunt down all who criticise you, and call those you hunt intolerant.

We've had enough!

Your utopias have lost all legitimacy for us.

Realise at last that we don't live in a unified world or in a global village. Wars, the poor, and the oppressed will always be with us. This world will never be a heaven on Earth.

Your delusions have only accomplished one thing: You have uprooted your children.

We are the lost, the homeless. 'Who are we?' we ask ourselves. 'Where are we going?'

We've seen through your answers and understood that they are lies. We aren't 'humanity' and we don't want your paradise.

So we have come up with our own answer to these questions.

We turn to what you have demonised. To ourselves.

We search for our identity, and find it under the rubble of your destructive rage. We must dig deep to find ourselves again.

Our history, our homeland, and our culture give us what you have taken from us.

We don't want to be citizens of the world. We are happier with our own countries.

We don't want the end of history, for our history doesn't give us cause to complain.

We don't want a multicultural society where our own culture is left to burn in the melting pot.

We are less demanding than you, yet we want so much more!

While you've chased utopias your entire lives, we want real values. What we demand actually exists; to possess it is our ancestral right. We desire nothing more than our inheritance, and won't tolerate your withholding it any longer.

We are the answer to you and to the failure of your utopia.

For we are generation identity.

2.

ON LONELINESS

We're a great riddle to you. An incomprehensible phenomenon.
Our words and deeds refute all your theories and arguments.
We live in the world you dreamt of, yet this world disgusts us.
Thanks to you, we could develop free from all social obligations and values; thanks to you we go lost and lonely through life.
You've destroyed everything that could have offered us identity and refuge, yet you're shocked that we're unhappy.
For deep in us lies a constant feeling of being alone, of being lost. We do everything to numb this feeling.
We throw the wildest parties and meet in glowing malls; we dance all night, take drugs, or hide behind our computers. Any means is justified in order to overcome this loneliness, but we are always still alone in the end.
You have taught us that we can buy anything. But where can we buy a remedy for loneliness?
Not that we didn't try. With brand names, labels, and the latest clothing styles, we want to belong to a certain group. It may seem laughable to you, but for us, this is one of the last remaining possibilities to somehow find a place where we belong.
Sometimes we manage to convince ourselves in our despair that we are absolutely unique, that we don't need to belong to anything. In this way we give ourselves strength when the loneliness overcomes us.

Even if, one day, we become part of a group, because our inner-most selves long for identity and belonging, we still can't enjoy it. We always hear your nagging voices in our heads, warning us about the dangers of peer pressure and the loss of our individuality. This inner conflict plunges us into yet deeper despair.

*

The dark companion of loneliness is boredom.

It's the boredom that first reveals how lonely we are. We don't ever want to be bored, because then we couldn't lie to ourselves anymore.

Yet boredom is our constant companion. It envelops us like a dark cloud and makes itself felt whenever we briefly pause from our frenzied searching.

This is why we seek to numb our boredom and loneliness, with means that become ever wilder and ever more reckless. But no artificial euphoria lasts long enough to bring us peace. No pleasure leads us to anything but desperate collapse.

So we wander through life, half-lost and half-high.

For we are generation identity.

3.

ON RELIGION

What is religion? What does the Church mean to us?

'There is no God' — that was your credo. Yet this claim is too radical for us.

Sometimes we believe in something, sometimes in nothing. A bit in God, a bit in biology, a bit in everything, and a bit in nothing.

That is our belief. We don't formulate it, or proclaim it, as you've twisted the profession of faith into something detestable. When we think of the Church, nothing but intolerance and backwardness come to mind.

We are not atheists. We believe in something. Yet this belief brings us no sense of belonging or of community. You've shut the welcoming arms of the Church to us once and for all.

*

Religious fanaticism in all of its forms is incomprehensible to us, and often seems primitive and stupid. Yet deeply religious people and cultures fascinate us, for we know they have something we lack: a deep, inner feeling that they are sheltered and protected. A lucid certainty in matters of right and wrong.

We can only imagine how it might feel not to be plagued by constant self-doubt. We will never feel that way ourselves, for religion has become unthinkable. We can't obey dogmas, and so we feel ourselves at once superior and inferior to the fanatics.

Every clear vow, every clear statement of faith appears crazed and closed-minded to us. Whenever someone appears ready to defend his beliefs, we suspect fanaticism and intolerance.

Yet even nothingness itself makes no sense to us. How are atheists supposed to know that there is no God? In this sense we believe in an indefinite higher power that may or may not exist.

*

Our belief is worthless, for we don't dare to take it seriously. Our fear of appearing fanatical is too great.

'I don't know' is our slogan, and with these words we plunge ourselves into misery.

We can't make ourselves believe anymore, and we therefore lack all orientation. Thus we go through life without being certain of anything, because we don't want to be certain of anything.

For we are generation identity.

4.

ON POLITICS

Sometimes we hear that there were once people who saw their highest honour in dedicating their lives to the service of the state.

We can't understand or relate to this, as you have made us loathe the state, rotting as it is from the inside.

You've demonised it as an instrument of oppression. You wanted to abolish the state by any means.

But you have failed. While all of you fought the state, the commonest and greediest among you seized control of it and became what today passes for politicians.

The rest of you turned away from government service, and thereby left politics to the most repulsive representatives of your generation. And so the government became nothing but another opportunity to make money for oneself and one's friends.

We bear the consequences of your failure. We pay the price for the fact that you were 'too good' to go into politics.

We don't hate the state, we despise it. But abolish it? That would never have occurred to us.

We are realists. We know that the state is a necessary evil.

We are pessimists. We don't expect anything but lies from politicians.

*

You went to vote bursting with enthusiasm, proud of your right to have a say. We can only laugh at your naïveté.

23

None of us still believes today that he can change something with his vote. We only vote if there's nothing good on TV.

The politicians of all the parties are the same to us. They all say the same thing, after all.

They promised the Moon. Unemployment, poverty, crime, and everything bad would be banished, if only we would vote for them. Except that as soon as they won, their words always turned out to be nothing but empty promises.

So we stopped voting. For as long as we can remember, we haven't cared which parties attempt to exploit us. The politicians are, for us, all the same old windbags without the slightest conception of the problems and worries of our generation.

*

You rule over us and run the political system only for yourselves. You don't care about the youth. And so we don't care about you. Leave us alone, and don't bother to try to act like our friends. We see through your grinning PR masks at first glance.

We don't want anything to do with you and your pathetic schemes, and you yourselves are the reason why. Your politics disgust us. Your scrabble for power and influence repels us. You repel us.

For we are generation identity.

5.

ON IDYLLIC FAMILY LIFE

In countless TV series you make us watch the lives of synthetically perfect families. We are hungry for such images, as they are the exact opposite of the reality you have brought into being.

In your unprecedented arrogance, you claimed that the family was no longer necessary. Father, mother, and child are supposedly an outdated model. You leapt gleefully to the task of stamping out the family.

That which should have been our place of refuge and source of inspiration became the stage for countless arguments and fights.

Your ideal was to enjoy success and the good life. And so you enjoyed life. But who watched out for your children?

You were egoists, and you divorced a thousand times without once thinking about what that would mean for us.

You wanted to have a career and to make money. So you moved to go wherever the best jobs were, and didn't give a thought to our welfare and stability.

You left us sitting alone in front of the TV, where the perfect life was presented to us every day. Full of rage, we compared our sad reality with the fantasy worlds into which we submerged ourselves.

*

A perpetual, deep resentment lies buried within us, as we know in our hearts that we were betrayed and tricked out of that which is most important. We can't articulate this resentment, but we take it out on you.

You often accuse us of acting irrationally—a justified accusation, as we don't act rationally, thoughtfully or logically.

We are the generation of the heart and of feeling, and our actions are determined by nothing other than a deep longing for the shelter you should have provided us.

The ideals of TV became *our* ideals. We have made them our own and we all dream of a wonderful family. This is what you threw away as old-fashioned and pointless; we want nothing more.

No one showed us how to build a family, or told us how to stick together or resolve a conflict. We have failed a thousand times in trying to realise our ideal.

Since you have run the economy into the ground, we must be 'flexible' and look for work wherever we can get it; it prevents us from realising our dream a million times over.

To pay for our pensions, we'll have to work more than all the generations before us; we know now that you'll even rob us of our future well-being, on top of everything else.

You rush across the globe to inject life into your dying economy and to delay paying back your debts, to keep your own pensions rolling in.

Yet our dream remains a happy family and future. However many roadblocks you put in our path, we won't give up this dream.

For we are generation identity.

6.

ON THE SEXES

Of all the battles you've fought, your battle against the sexes was the most reprehensible.

Instead of the harmonious union of men and women, you've promoted alliances of queers and transvestites, the union of nothingness.

You've taken the manliness out of men. You've raised them to be feeble teddy bears lacking the power to act, lacking courage, lacking strength — in short, the will to power.

You've convinced women that femininity is outdated and socially constructed. You've told them that it's not necessary to look pretty and healthy, not necessary to have families and children, and that only their careers matter.

So it was that the womanly men and the manly women met, and didn't know what to do.

We won't repeat your mistakes. We shake our heads at your imbecile theories, and want to be masculine men and feminine women. It may appear old-school and outdated to you, but we like it that way.

Women *want* to be conquered. The longing for the one who can win them over and make them his lies deep in them.

Instead of heroic knights, you send them 'good friends' and feeble cowards.

Men *want* to win a woman who is worth the effort and the trials they must endure, for whom the leap through the fire and the battle with the dragon are worth it.

27

Today, instead of the beautiful princess, only a scowling feminist or a jutting manjaw awaits the hero at the end.

We've recognised the true nature of the sexes, and we want to live in harmony with it. We want to be real men and real women.

For we are generation identity.

7.

ON THE UNBORN CHILDREN

It's time to give speech to the speechless. What would those who have never spoken a word have said to you? What do they think, those who never had a chance to think?

Perhaps you can already guess of whom I speak. I mean the unborn children, the murdered and unwanted. I speak of the brothers and sisters who should be standing at our sides. Of our dead siblings.

*

We are the too-few generation of the single children. Therein lies the source of our loneliness. You have slaughtered our siblings.

You committed murder by the millions and euphemised your crime with words like 'sexual emancipation' and 'family planning.' What you call abortion, we call murder.

Your egoism and presumptuousness knew no bounds. You really believed that you could appoint yourselves to be the judges of life and death.

So spoke your 'law,' and if having a child was inconvenient at that moment, you killed it. In this way, you robbed countless children of their lives to arrange yours more pleasantly.

But what could be a greater crime than the murder of unborn children?

*

We mourn our dead siblings. We miss them, even if we never met them. We call to them, 'Brothers and sisters! Our beloved, murdered siblings! Forgive your murderers, for they know not what they do.'

But we know what we are doing. We are those who have survived your cleansing, and we also fight for the lives of future children.

We will put an end to your mass murder.

For we are generation identity.

8.

ON THE ECONOMY

Despite all your failures, one would have hoped that you would at least have the economy under control. Weren't perpetual growth and riches what you strived for? Didn't you want to achieve the greatest possible prosperity?

And yet you've smashed the economy to pieces. And you leave it to us to try and put this pile of rubble back together again.

*

You were greedy and exorbitant in all respects. Greed and indulgence drove your 'economic planning.'

Low unemployment, low taxes, and maximal social security—you truly enjoyed a life of excess. Half of what you spent you earned, the rest you embezzled.

To maintain your standard of living, you increase your debts year by year.

You record the growing debts, but do nothing; it doesn't perturb you in the least.

Of course you've always complained about it, but never fought to stop it.

This is because it is not really your problem. You always knew that someone else would have to pay your debts. That we would have to pay them off.

But one day the debts grew so big that your bank wouldn't loan you more money. Then you called for rescue, knowing that the economy would collapse without fresh infusions of cash. Unemployment rose, but you weren't the ones to pay the price. We do, the younger generation, who can't find a job. We are the ones forced to sacrifice to pay off your mountain of debt.

*

You could complete your studies secure in the knowledge that, diploma in hand, you would never want for work. We get two degrees, and call ourselves happy if we can get a temp job afterwards.

Once again we pay for your mistakes.

You believed in progress, that your wealth would continue to grow forever. We celebrate every day that we don't grow poorer.

Europe's and America's economies are shutting down, and we no longer believe they will recover. For you the crisis is the exception; for us it is the rule.

We are unemployed, poorly paid, or work 60-hour weeks. We are the victims of your debt-driven politics.

For we are generation identity.

9.

ON CRITICAL THINKING

If you've taught us one thing, it's that we should not, and may not, believe in anything. We've learned this lesson much more thoroughly than you realize.

Question, criticise, and doubt everything—so you lectured us. And when you said 'everything,' you meant, above all, the old values of family, tradition, and country.

We followed your lead, criticising, questioning, and doubting everything. But when we say 'everything,' we truly mean everything. Above all, we mean you.

Did you really think that the generation you raised in total doubt would follow in your footsteps? Did you really believe that we would accept your critique of all values uncritically? Did you really think that we would continue your work of destruction, just because you told us how? How little you know your own children!

The critical minds among us were the first to see through your smokescreen. We listened sceptically to your hollow phrases about tolerance and emancipation, and yet we didn't let your wishful thinking throw sand in our eyes. Our gaze penetrated the obscuring fog of your mental confusion and saw things as they are.

We watch your dead ideas and laughable hallucinations writhe on the ground, gasping for breath, waiting for someone to deal them the mercy blow.

We're glad to assume the task, and to finally bring peace, to you as well.

We'll carry you carefully onwards, and lay you down to rest. Sleep, dear parents. Stop trying to influence politics. Stop trying to adapt reality to your false dreams. Take a rest; you've truly done enough.

Do not worry. Know that the world is in good hands. We will destroy the monsters you have created. We will make your barren land bear fruit again. The society you tried to liberate by destroying it, we will rebuild.

Rest. Leave the task of shaping Europe to those who know something about it. Leave it to us.

Step down and make room.

For generation identity.

10.

ON ECOLOGY

You've said often and at great length that we must fight — against the destruction of our planet, climate change, nuclear energy and the destruction of the rainforest.

You've given great speeches, and made yourselves feel important. You've said and announced everything imaginable, but you haven't protected the environment.

One must ask: why have you failed? Why were all your words and intentions useless?

It is the same with everything you do. You also *wanted* to create a functioning multicultural society, but you couldn't, because your goal was unrealistic. And although the goal of a sustainable world is realistic, your supposed path was an imaginary one.

Did you really believe that you could save the environment by chaining yourselves to trees? What do demonstrations in Europe *really* do for the rainforest?

You never thought about the results of your actions. You just wanted to quiet your conscience and play at being rebels. A real solution for our planet would have naturally required thorough, thought-out plans and concrete strategies.

But that would have been too strenuous for you. You preferred to blame politics and the economy for your manifest negligence. As you never thought of taking realistic steps, you left the protection of our planet to the most ineffectual dreamers and quacks.

The Greens, the biggest pack of nuts among your generation, were the only ones who truly fought the battle for the Earth.

They, however, discredited the fight with their own repulsive behaviour, associating it with drug use and the like.

Environmental protection is too important to be left to fantasists, yet you let the biggest fantasists of all hijack the debate.

So it came to be that the fight for the Earth had no clear organisation or structure; essentially none of the ingredients for success.

*

Here you failed in another critical area. Have you done anything right? Watch us and learn how one really protects the environment, without big demonstrations and blowing up factories. In fact, real environmental protection doesn't even stop one from showering.

Resolute and earnest, we will save the planet.

For we are generation identity.

11.

ON THE MULTICULTURAL SOCIETY

All earthly things appear quite different to different observers. That which each observer expects and hopes for clouds and alters his perception. Our previous experiences change our view of the world, and to speak of you, ideologies, hallucinations and other fantasies have darkened your vision of the true nature of things.

It may be that two people see the same thing entirely differently, on account of their different experiences and preconceived notions.

It may just as well be that two generations see the same matter entirely differently.

So it is between us and you regarding your multicultural society.

*

Decades ago you carried the torch for multiculturalism and wanted to implement it at any cost. But what does multiculturalism mean to you? Nothing more than eating pizza and kebabs at the Turkish joint. Other than that, you have precious little to do with the multicultural society. And because you like to eat Turkish food and don't quite get what's going on, it's easy for you to damn our criticisms as 'prejudice.' In your perception, multiculturalism is working quite fine.

But your children see things a bit differently. We go to class with 80% or more foreign-born students. Knife-mad Turks, drug-dealing Africans, and fanatical Muslims. Your cheap clichés are our reality.

That is why we hate your great dream of the multicultural society. What do you know about this society? Nothing.

So stop trying to lecture us. Stop trying to sell us the line that we're evil racists, just because your utopia disgusts us.

Don't come at us with the Second World War and Hitler when we're talking about Mehmed the Conqueror and Mustafa. And don't tell us that foreigners are exactly like us, when we see every day that they're not.

*

We are more disenfranchised than they are. We don't want Mehmed and Mustafa to become Europeans. We don't want immigrants to take over our identities and give up their own.

They should hold on to their own identities, and let us have ours. We don't ask more than that which should be obvious: Europe belongs to the Europeans alone. We are the rightful heirs to this continent, and we will not give up our inheritance.

For we are generation identity.

12.

ON UNIVERSALISM

Do you ever ask yourselves what the future will think of you? If statues will be built to commemorate your shining example? How they will judge your deeds and actions?

You clearly haven't. If you'd even once thought about how posterity will judge you, even once briefly paused and thought of the future, it would have occurred to you that your children and grandchildren will spit your names in disgust. They will not continue your work of destruction.

*

But don't worry, you don't need to wait until the future to find people whose hatred you thoroughly earned. You don't even need to speak with your children. It's enough if you just once leave the West and go out into the wider world.

Outside of your emancipated societies there are still other cultures and peoples. They cast a wary eye on your utopias.

Can you even imagine such a thing? Can you even entertain the thought that some societies don't want you to 'liberate' them?

How could that be? You've brought all the wonders of Western civilisation with you! With capitalism, democracy, and human rights in your suitcase, you set off on your liberation tour.

Growing curious, you question the members of other peoples about their cultures. But as soon as they start to answer, you break in and explain how they can improve their cultures and become more like you.

We hate your hypocritical xenophilia with a passion. You offer one hand to these cultures in peace; in the other you hold the knife. And yet all the while, you still believe you are doing good.

*

The rest of the world hates you. Do you have the slightest clue why? Do you have any idea why the rest of the world regards you with such hostility? Not because you exploit or dominate them militarily. This belongs to the great and eternal game of peoples, in which each seeks its advantage. No, the world hates you for your hypocrisy.

Not even history's greatest imperialists were half as arrogant as you. The imperialists may have robbed and enslaved the world, but at least they never pretended to be the good ones, bringing peace and freedom. They were out for profit, and freely admitted it.

But you want to save the world. To bring the world democracy, human rights, and capitalism. You try to modernise the world, and to force your false modernity and arrogant notions of progress upon everyone you encounter. Nothing insults and offends the proud and ancient cultures of India, China, Russia, Persia, and so many other lands more than your crusades to teach and 'improve' them.

*

You've buried Europe's culture, and now you want to annihilate all the others. The world will never forgive you for this arrogance.

We, your children, can imagine their hate quite well. Who knows better than us how it feels to be patronised by you? We know the feeling of being uprooted and set adrift. So it is that we understand the peoples who despise you and reject your 'progress.'

For we are generation identity.

13.

ON DEMOCRACY

Superficially it would appear that both our generations stand for at least one common cause. At least on one point we seem to agree: in our passionate commitment to the principle of the rule of the people, democracy.

In the end, however, we agree on nothing more than a word. It becomes clear soon enough that we understand something entirely different by the word democracy.

When we think of democracy, the image of Athens and the right to participate in the community's decisions come to mind. We strongly believe that the people have a right not only to participate in these decisions, but to make them entirely of their own accord.

Direct democracy and referenda are our ideals. When we say democracy, we *really* mean democracy.

*

Your understanding of democracy, on the other hand, is just as hypocritical as everything else about you. Sure, you claim to believe in the principle of the rule of the people, and consider yourselves to be good, democratic citizens. In reality, however, your words are empty and devoid of all content.

You refuse to allow the people to vote about the things that really matter. You fear 'populism' you say—this is what you call views other than your own—and the 'stupidity' of the people.

The people supposedly doesn't know anything about the essential questions.

We claim, however, that the people can make judgments in decisive matters a thousand times better than your elected representatives, who live in an ideological bubble.

*

Why are you afraid of the people? Why do you shudder with fear in the face of the idea of referenda? Perhaps because you know that the majority of Europeans don't share your opinion? Because you know that they would shoot down your political strategy, and gladly watch it go down in flames?

You've always confined yourselves to the universities and the nation's intellectual and cultural elite. Using this elite you wanted to implement your psychotic schemes; the people was always only a stumbling block.

But we put more faith in Europeans than you. Even if they don't share our opinions on all points, we know we will persuade them and bring them over to our side.

We come from the people, and we fight for the people and their right to decide their own political destiny. We demand real democracy. We're not afraid of the will of the Europeans.

For we are generation identity.

14.

ON DIVERSITY

Colourful, diverse, heterogeneous; you sure like to sell yourselves as proponents of diversity. You tolerate every perversion and think that by doing so that you're doing diversity a service. Yet you're wrong once again.

A picture doesn't take on vivid contrasts when one mixes all the colours together, but when one paints each colour in its respective place.

Large-scale diversity requires small-scale homogeneity.

*

You can't grasp this. You see one multicultural metropolis, and you want every city to become like it. You speak of diversity, but you want to make everything the same.

Don't you preach it to us every day?

There has to be *one* market, you claim. *One* form of government is the right one. You want to implement *one* formulation of human rights, which should apply to *everyone*. We all live in *one* world. These are your slogans. How is it then that you dare to claim that you stand for diversity, when you hate diversity from the depths of your being?

*

We don't want to see one and the same kind of city spread across the entire world. We want to travel to other countries and experience entirely *different* cultures, not further outposts of a universal, globalised metropolis.

We want to return home to our own culture, where we feel in harmony with ourselves, not to a cookie-cutter colony of conformity to a multicultural empire.

*

We oppose your credo of multiculturalism with the principle of ethnopluralism. Instead of mixing and standardisation, we want to preserve difference. We want different peoples, cultures, and identities. Our own included!

We want the world to remain a colourfully vibrant and enchanting mosaic; we don't want a drab, grey projection screen. We are the real representatives of diversity; its real guerrilla warriors.

For we are generation identity.

15.

ON NATIONAL SOCIALISM

We haven't gone easy on you in some regards. We've pitilessly criticised your failures, and yet it is clear to us why you came to make these failures in the first place.

We know what first planted these sick hypotheses about a multicultural, emancipated, and de-gendered society in your heads. It was National Socialism.

*

You were born after the war. You've seen the rubble from the destruction and heard the reports first-hand. The horror and devastation left behind by the rule of the National Socialists left a deep mark on you.

So it was that you wanted to do the opposite of the Nazis in all respects. Where there was something to which they said yes, you uncritically said no, without once thinking about the actual question.

*

National Socialism determined your entire thinking. No one shaped your worldview more than Adolf Hitler.

Nazism was racist, so you wanted to be 'anti-racist.' Nazism was nationalist? Naturally, you became internationalist. It was militaristic, fascistic, and imperialistic, and so you became anti-military, anti-fascist and anti-imperialist. If Nazism promoted a belief in the traditional family, you had to damn that as well.

In this way, Adolf Hitler became your greatest role model.

Your efforts to reject the extremist ideology of National Socialism led you to create your own extremist ideology. Fanatically believing that you were doing the right thing, you set out to lay waste to Europe.

*

We, however, enjoy greater intellectual freedom than you. We are the first generation after 1933 to have truly overcome National Socialism. We neither define ourselves in terms of it, nor in terms of opposing it. We reject its ideology and hostility to the freedom and the diversity of peoples, just as we reject your ideology.

What does the Second World War mean for us? We've learned from its story that we Europeans shouldn't fight one another over petty disagreements. You have also taught us that we Europeans shouldn't hate ourselves for petty reasons.

We don't damn and demonise. We learn. You've failed to learn from the 'Third Reich,' and have become just as extremist as the National Socialists. Unlike you, we can justly and rightly claim to have overcome National Socialism. We toss both it and your sick ideas where they belong, into the rubbish bin of history.

For we are generation identity.

16.

ON THE END OF THE WORLD

Your fear of the End of Days has been considerable of late. Even if you don't believe in old Mayan inscriptions, you shudder at the thought of them. Do you fear death? Does it strike fear into your hearts that volcanoes will rise out of the Earth, and that lava will turn your cities to ash?

You fools! We are already in the middle of the end!

Your dull dispositions, filed down and flattened by Hollywood films, make you blind to everything that doesn't explode in your face.

You don't need to study the Mayan prophecies to see the end coming. You just need to open your eyes.

Our Earth is dying; she is bleeding from a million wounds. Every single day, earth-movers and bulldozers transform our colourful planet, piece by piece, into a lifeless desert. Take a look at the rainforests and oceans; seek the oil rigs and petrol pumps, and you will find death.

You've taken everything away, robbed everything of its worth; you have no scruples about killing the mother us all.

Yet deep inside you can surely guess that your sins will catch up with you, that you were too greedy and immoderate. You are enthused by films about catastrophe and destruction, because you know that one day nature will have its revenge. And this may happen simply because its bounty may one day not be there anymore.

Perhaps then you will grasp that not everything is worthless. That it is sensible to think of the future. And that humanity would rather live a bit less extravagantly in order to live a thousand times longer.

Look at the images of our ruined planet and ask yourselves: was it really worth it?

*

But don't cause yourself any worries; you won't experience the real and final consequences of your destructive rage. You'll be long gone, and it will be up to us to set out on a new path. We will depart from your path of destruction, and live in harmony and respect for nature. Perhaps not as richly and luxuriously as you, and yet considerably happier.

For we are generation identity.

17.

ON FOREIGN AFFAIRS

In your speeches and texts, you always announce great things and glorious deeds, but in reality, you are sorely lacking in them. If you were heroes in theory, the praxis always saw you with your heads firmly planted in the sand.

This is above all the case in questions of European foreign policy. Where braver and heartier men were called for, you stood as loudmouths and cowards. For decades, you allowed Europe to become the willing servant of America.

Becoming a servant, you always had to come when the bell was rung.

Of course you did it with a scowl, but you did it nonetheless. It never occurred to you that you might work out your own political program.

*

This arrangement was, for you, by no means a bad set-up. American armies defended Europe and attacked everyone who threatened Europe, or who the Americans claimed to be doing so.

You could stand by and point accusingly at the murdering Americans, while at the same time being glad that they took the fighting off your hands. Despite your hypocritical rejection of the Americans, you still remain in an alliance with them.

What they demanded in return, namely the participation of European soldiers in American crusades, seemed to you a reasonable price. So it was that the sons of Europe died in lands where they had no business being in the first place.

*

But the times change, America is turning its focus to the Pacific theatre, where it is stepping up to challenge its new competitor, China.

The great battles of our time will be fought in Asia, and on the wide Pacific Ocean, where these two Titans come to meet.

The Americans are gradually withdrawing from Europe, as their power doesn't suffice to dominate the entire world. 'Defend yourselves!' they cry out to us as they leave.

*

We therefore stand before a tremendous challenge, too great for you. If Europe is threatened in the future, it will need to defend itself.

Can you still fight at all, can you kill if need be? Do you even know how to defend yourselves at all?

You don't, because you'd rather lead Europe to its downfall than condescend to defend it.

But we know what we have to do. We are ready to defend our continent in times of crisis.

Here we stand before mighty tasks. NATO has long passed its expiration date.

America won't help us in the future, and we identitarian Europeans have no interest in fighting America's battles. It's therefore up to us to find a new way.

Europe needs its own army. A capable and organised fighting force, whose goal is not the invasion of other countries, but the protection of European neutrality on a global scale.

That which Switzerland is to Europe, Europe must become to the world. A strong and independent region that attacks no one, and that no one dares to attack.

*

You've let yourselves be used by the USA, and in doing so weren't any better than common whores. Self-assured and brave, we will declare to the world: 'No European will die for a foreign nation, and no enemy can ever hope to conquer Europe.'

This is our message to the world.

For we are generation identity.

18.

ON THE EUROPEAN UNION

A united Europe. That is what all Europeans need and want. Let us never again fight among one another. Never again fall into the bloodlust that twice pushed our continent to the precipice of total annihilation.

We all agree on this point. But as in all things, you have failed us in the unification of Europe.

You didn't show the slightest foresight when you structured this continent politically, and your entire strategy remained incomplete. A half-job, without vision and passion.

As you were lacking any plan, any will to a great political leap, business and finance took the reins of the project of building a united Europe.

When business gets involved in politics, however, the result is seldom good, not in economic nor in other matters.

Nonetheless, you allowed the short-term interests of a few to trump the long-term interests of all. Lobbying groups and international firms called the shots and built that which we now call the European Union.

It's an organisation without any democracy whatsoever. It has no unity, and its decisions are not consensual. It is the rule of lobbyism in its purest form.

*

The construction of Europe would be easy if one only had the courage to think things through to the end. That you don't is painfully obvious.

We want to tell you, therefore, what possibilities were open to you from the very beginning. You could have taken either of the following paths instead:

You could have preserved the ability of the European nation-states to retain their sovereignty, and created a European common market and a European alliance while doing without European regulations, a common currency, and a European Parliament. Briefly: you could have created a united Europe of free fatherlands.

The other possibility would have been the creation of a European state. General, Europe-wide elections and parties and a truly European government, that is to say, a powerful and effective centralised state.

These were your two options, each with its own advantages and disadvantages.

You've managed to combine the worst of each.

You've robbed the nation-states of their sovereign powers without transferring these powers to the European level.

So it is that the nation-states aren't allowed to decide many things that the European Union itself can't do, because it can only act with the consent of all member states.

Neither a confederation of states nor a centralised state, the current European Union is a failed project that *must* dramatically collapse in the face of the first half-serious challenge.

*

It's up to us to build, out of the rubble of this crisis, a new and upright Europe. A Europe that decides what it wants, and isn't the incompetent tool of corporations.

We want to build the Europe that our glorious continent deserves. Your EU is an insult to us.

For we are generation identity.

19.

ON DEATH

Once humans believed they were like leaves on a tree: leaves that grew, flourished, and one day wilted, fell to the ground, and in turn nourished the tree.

Humanity believed it was part of a whole, a branch on the tree of the world. An integral part of the eternal Being and Becoming.

The peoples of the world invented the most varied religions, gods and philosophies to express this ancient belief.

You were the first to scorn this belief that we are all parts of a whole.

This theory seemed unnecessary to you. What is more, it didn't fit into your concept of a self-determined individual.

So you went through life not bothering about anyone other than yourselves.

And truly, you knew how to live! No generation before you had tasted all the pleasures of life as you did.

But do you mighty heroes of pleasure and excess also know how to die? Can you steel yourselves for the end? What will you feel when the cold hand of death reaches for you?

*

We are certain that you don't understand the meaning of this question. In reality, one can't even expect it of you. So we want to explain it to you.

When it comes to death, only two things matter. Firstly: *how* does one die? And secondly: *for what?*

You still don't understand the question? Let us explain to you as we would to children:

One can accept death and see it as the beginning of eternal life, and so pass joyfully into the whole. One can, on the other hand, miserably retreat, clinging with all one's power to the last vestiges of one's existence, and attempt to drag out the bitter end.

You choose the latter with a vengeance.

We, however, want to spare ourselves this pitiful spectacle. Neither the way you live nor the way you die appeals to us.

This was the question of 'how'; now we want to explain the question of what one should die *for*.

To die for something. We can truly see how this phrase makes you visibly uncomfortable. Nothing could appear more absurd to you, who only believe in your own lives, as the idea that you should give this life away *for* something.

*

We ourselves don't want to preach a false fatalism. It isn't our goal to die as soon as possible, and yet we would do it, if necessary, for certain causes.

But what would you die for? For what would you give your life away? Can you even answer this question for yourselves? Consider the following:

He who has no reason to die, has no reason to live.

We don't want to die, but are ready to do so. For our family, our country, for everything that makes us what we are, without which we could no longer be ourselves. For our identity. In this way, our lives are not lived pointlessly and in vain. As parts of the whole, we will rejoin the whole once again.

For we are generation identity.

20.

ON SEXUALITY

Truly, it requires great boldness to broach this theme. We're often accused, and often correctly, of being the generation of sexual permissiveness. The generation without values, principles, or meaningful relationships. Yes! All of these accusations are justified. Yet they are only one side of the coin, and in the end, whoever accuses the youth of a lack of sexual inhibitions without illuminating its causes has as little of an understanding of the youth as he does of sexuality.

We reject unrestrained sexuality more than any other generation. This is because for no previous generation in history has true love played such a great role as it does for us.

Of all the things that you're devalued and destroyed, you've left us love. Truly, you've never really cared about love. You've despised it and sold it short. But precisely for that reason, you've never launched a frontal assault against it. It remained alive.

And it became to our last place of refuge.

So here we are in this world of loneliness and fleeting happiness; we long for the person who can bring us to safety. It is our highest goal and our greatest happiness to find true love.

*

Yet we are sexually promiscuous, drink hard, and settle for the second best. No one suffers more from this than we ourselves.

Two powerful drives rage within us—the longing for true love on the one hand, and wild animal desire on the other.

Only a few happy ones among us succeed in fusing these two fundamental forces together. The great majority, however, find themselves in a relentless and pitiless combat with themselves. You fired the first shot in this war.

The consequences of your 'sexual liberation' have us in a stranglehold. It is impossible to go out for even a day into the world without being greeted by half-naked men and women. All films, advertising, and magazines consciously manipulate sexual desire. So it is that desire grows, often in opposition to our love. When it's over and the wild, alcohol-soaked night is behind us, we regret what we've done. Often we feel sad because of it.

*

This inner struggle, which each of us must win for himself, is also part of our identity.

Yet we declare resolutely: we want to win it! A long road may lie before us, but in the end, the love within us will triumph over animalistic desire.

For we are generation identity.

21.

ON RACISM

You've got cause to rejoice, as we have now come to the word you like to say the most. And about the people you hate the most. About racism and racists, who spread their racist ideology in the most racist of ways.

You don't quite want to specify exactly what this racism is supposed to be. And why would you? If there was a clear definition, you couldn't accuse *everyone* you don't like of racism.

*

In the past there were people who identified themselves as racists, and called for the classification of humanity according to genetic characteristics such as the shape of noses and eye colour.

Today, however, no one speaks of such things, the only exception being you.

No one thinks about race any more, but you continue to hunt for racists as if possessed, since you claim to find hidden racism everywhere.

We all reject racism. No one, neither you nor us, desire that people should be discriminated against or oppressed because of their genetic heritage.

We limit ourselves to rejecting racism as such. But you want to designate all of your political opponents, including us, as racists.

Our clear affirmation of European identity, culture, and tradition, our will to keep Europe alive, and our resolve to not be the last European generation, are all thorns in your side.

You seek to avenge yourselves by interpreting our affirmation of life and of Europe as racism.

*

But is everyone who believes that there are different peoples, cultures, and identities, and that this is *good*, really a racist?

We won't let this label stick on *us*!

If you smear every affirmation of one's own identity with accusations of racism, then everyone is a racist, always was a racist, and will always be a racist. Even you are no exception to this rule.

Yes, we could even accuse you of racism. Only in this way could one explain your pathological hatred of Europe.

We, however, are no racists. Nor are we as preoccupied with race and racism as you are. We make our own choices and go our own ways, without paying any attention to your baseless accusations.

For we are generation identity.

22.

ON THE NEW YEAR

Soon fireworks will paint the heavens with fountains of radiant light across the world. Tracing their fiery paths across the night sky, they greet the new year with a bang.

The new year will be celebrated all over the world, and in many places, there is good reason to do so.

The Chinese and the Indians are celebrating the births of their new, powerful economies. The new year is yet another that will bring them closer to the golden future which these great civilisations have rightly earned.

The Americans celebrate their world power, and hope to hold on to it for a long time to come.

The Africans celebrate their future, for in their view, the new year can only be better than the last.

The Middle East celebrates its hard-won victories and revolutions, and hopes for further victories in honour and praise of its God.

*

But what should Europeans celebrate? What reason does Europe have to look forward to the future? What good could the new year bring to our sick and weak continent?

Yet Europe celebrates, with all the flash and colour of the rest of the world.

But our celebrations appear fake and tired. They resemble the birthday parties of an old man who is simply happy to have lived another year, but who has no more plans for the future.

Europe is sick. Poisoned by you and your ideologies, its vital functions are shutting down.

What future should a culture without children celebrate? What do peoples who will soon be minorities in their own countries have to celebrate?

Yet Europe celebrates. Everything glows and burns, and so we manage to imagine, at least for this one day, that our continent, perhaps, has a future after all.

*

Did the ancient Romans also celebrate the new year? They did indeed!

In the last days of the Empire — as no real government remained, the Germans were pouring in, and the power of the state existed only on paper — the Romans drank their wine, toasting to the future and to their great civilisation.

The ability to close one's eyes to unpleasant realities isn't unique to you.

But we don't close our eyes. We recognise the problems and the threats, and do everything to ward them off. We are laying the foundation for a European future. In time, we will give Europe a new reason to celebrate the coming of a new year. If there is any cause to celebrate the new year and smile upon the future, it is us.

For we are generation identity.

23.

ON THE DECLINE AND FALL OF THE ROMAN EMPIRE

As the Visigoths crossed the Danube in 376 and penetrated the borders of the Eastern Roman Empire, Emperor Valens was facing a fateful decision. His generals pleaded with him to gather the army and force back the Goths. His political advisers, however, feared a long and bitter war. In their view, the Visigoths were only defenceless refugees displaced by the Huns. They convinced Valens that he must show compassion, and assign the Goths land in the Roman Empire. The Empire had far too few soldiers, so it might be quite clever to win the Visigoths as allies. What was wrong with taking them in? In fifty years, so they thought, the Visigoths would be civilised Roman citizens like all the rest. Only their unusually pale skin and blonde hair would remain as reminders that they came from outside.

So they gave the Visigoths land. Some years went by, and the Romans congratulated themselves on their brilliant solution to the problem. They drank their wine and let the Visigoths fight for them.

Yet the Visigoths did not by any means integrate themselves into Roman society, but became a state within the state. Over the course of the following years, ever more Germanic peoples crossed the Danube and joined the Visigoths. The power of the tribe became so mighty that it no longer followed the Emperor's orders.

When Emperor Valens recognised that the Visigoths had grown out of his control, he sent his army to subdue them. But there were already far too many of them. The Romans underestimated the power of the Visigoths and were defeated.

Thereafter, fleeing from the Huns, the tribe murdered and pillaged its way through the whole Empire. In 410 they sacked Rome, and finally settled in Gaul.

The Huns were now a Western Roman problem. After having recovered their strength and won a victory over the Goths, the Romans once again faced the question: should we continue the attack and drive them back to Germania, or ally ourselves with them?

Fearing a long war, the Roman politicians sent the Goths enormous quantities of gold to win them as allies against the Huns.

When the Hunnic Empire finally collapsed after Attila's death, the Roman treasury was bare. The countryside had been ravaged or occupied by the Visigoths and other Germanic tribes.

Money for new soldiers was lacking, and although the external threat from the Huns had been eliminated, the Empire was still doomed to fall. Vandals, Alemanni, and Visigoths were firmly established within the Empire, and could no longer be removed. The Romans sent them gold to purchase peace, but at some point their reserves ran out. Then the Germanic tribes finally declared independence from Rome and laid waste to the rest of the Western Empire. In 476, the last Emperor of Rome was dethroned.

*

The fall of the Roman Empire is similar to the process now underway in Europe. Will we one day speak of the decline and fall of the West?

*

Devastated and weakened by the Second World War, allegedly clever European politicians sought help from outside. The borders were opened to millions of Muslims, intended to breathe new life into a Europe with a declining birth rate and allow Europe to compete economically with the USA and the Soviet Union and, later, with the rising powers such as China and India.

The Muslims, however, didn't integrate themselves, but formed parallel societies. They had significantly more children than Europeans; their numbers grew without pause through new births and continued immigration.

The politicians sought to keep them quiet with payoffs from the welfare state, but in the course of an overwhelming economic crisis, their savings gave out. Europe had to start making cuts, and so unrest began among the immigrants, first in 2005 in Paris, then in 2011, starting in London, and spreading across England.

The number of Muslims continued to grow, and at a certain point, they began to dominate the state and civil society. When the Europeans finally attempted to rise up against them, their rebellion was suppressed. The Europeans, having grown old and weak, had nothing with which they could oppose the young and strong Muslims. Western civilisation dissolved, and new Muslim empires emerged on its former territory.

*

We can still prevent this future. We can still bring about a change of events. Yet we can only do this if we honestly and pitilessly admit to ourselves what sort of a situation we are actually in.

We have the courage to do this. With the example of the Romans before us, we know that we will need to fight for our identity.

Europe's fate is not yet sealed, and we ourselves will write our history!

For we are generation identity.

25.

ON ISLAM

No power in this world presents more of an obstacle to your 'emancipated' global village than Islam.

The East turned against you with all of its power and strength, and challenged the West.

The Muslims opposed your fanatical and heedless ideology with an equally fanatical religion, the political Islam.

You thought that by bringing your message to the East and the Muslim world, you would be greeted as the bearers of good tidings. You thought you would bring the Muslims to Europe in order to 'enlighten' and 'educate' them.

You were convinced that the Muslims would modernise and reform their religion. Yet they did the exact opposite.

The more righteously you spread the gospel of democracy and human rights, the stronger the resistance against you grew. The more Muslims got to know your liberated society, the more they rejected it.

They didn't reform Islam, they radicalised it.

Today millions of Muslims live in Europe and laugh at your ideology with contempt. You still hope to be able to win them over. You call this integration. Yet it's time to recognise one thing: the proud Muslims of the East will never accept your beliefs and theories.

That would mean that they would have to give up their identities. And they are far from doing so.

*

In fact, the situation is quite the opposite. For some time now, the most radical of the Muslims, also known as the Salafists, have been on an aggressive counteroffensive. They are proselytising in the heart of Europe. Among the uprooted and disoriented Europeans, there are a few who apparently find Islam an anchor in the storm.

So it is that these two fanatical ideologies square off in combat: political Islam versus the ideology of the '68ers. They mutually accuse one another of being the embodiment of absolute evil. We, the identitarian generation, stand in the crossfire of this battle.

*

We don't commit the error of many conservatives who declare Islam to be their absolute enemy. We don't believe that one should try and convert Muslims to so-called 'Western values' — quite the opposite! We neither want to disturb the identity of Muslims, nor do we want to launch crusades against the East as you did.

We condemn neither Muslims nor Islam. Here we are a thousand times more tolerant than you ever were. We neither hate nor demonise. We don't claim to have found the absolute truth, but recognise the unique and legitimate truths of each and every culture.

Yet in some matters, we brook no argument.

The presence of millions of Muslims in Europe represents a continuing threat to the peace of our continent. Not because the Muslims are the embodiment of pure evil, but because your multicultural society doesn't work.

*

The question of Islam is one of the great questions of our time. We will answer it and succeed where you have always failed. We will find a solution.

For we are generation identity.

25.

ON BODY AND MIND

For centuries, all philosophies and religions taught the unity of body and mind. He who seeks to scale intellectual peaks must also keep his body healthy and pure, so the teaching went.

Yet you have abolished this unity. You despised physical health and explained that the natural desire for a healthy and strong body was only a trick of advertising and fashion magazines. That sort of thinking is supposedly old-fashioned; everyone should be satisfied with how he is.

With these pretty words you corrupted us, your children.

*

Thrown into a world of excess, our generation has lost sight of what it means to fight. You yourselves didn't consider it necessary for us to be brought up to be hard, nor to be hard with ourselves.

As a consequence we have become soft and weak. Many of us were already overweight and lazy as children, yet instead of helping these children, playing sports with them and showing them the beauty of physical fitness, you made them believe that poisoning their own bodies was all right.

You even handed them the poison in a silver spoon. In the sincere belief that you were doing something good for your children, you brought them the greatest misery.

Just like a dog that isn't allowed to run or an eagle that is kept from flying, a human who doesn't use his body can never be satisfied.

Many of us have recognised that neglecting the body and sports has made us sick, and that fatty food, sugary snacks, and non-stop television leave us unhealthy.

In our resolve to overcome your absurd ideas, we reconstructed the unity of mind and body.

As we search for our identity, we want to become hard again. We don't want to be soft and posh anymore. We want to be strong and happy. We want to experience the world through sweat and ravenous gulps of fresh air, not to have it presented to us on the sofa.

*

We dive into ice-cold rivers, climb the highest mountains, and run until our strength gives out.

For we are generation identity.

26.

ON FREEDOM

Freedom is the greatest good in European thought. We fought wars, ignited revolutions, and toppled kings and dictators for freedom. We were executed for freedom and spilled our blood in her name. She intoxicated us and gave us the courage to perform great deeds. For freedom is our most passionate love. No other held us under such a spell.

*

But you have abused her. You've disgraced her name and painted your work of destruction as *her* will.

You truly believed you stood for freedom. Yet you knew nothing of her.

'What can we free ourselves from?' was your question. So you turned against everything that tried to influence you and destroyed it.

You smashed family, culture, country, tradition, the sexes, and a thousand other things. You cut all your ties with them in order to be 'free.' And now you are. Yet it is impossible for you to grasp that we, your children, intentionally turn toward the ties that you cut.

*

We have recognised that your question was wrong from the very start.

'Free from what?' you asked. Your answer was, 'Free from everything!' And so you stood alone at the end.

But we ask, 'Free *for* what?' And our answer is, 'Free to find our way back to ourselves.'

In the first instance, we ask ourselves: 'What do we want to do? What do we believe in? What do we fight for?' Only when we have defined our goals can we recognise what holds us back and what we need to free ourselves from.

So we came to a decision:

We want our identity back. We want everything back that you destroyed. But you, your ideas, your accusations and criticism, stand between us and our identity.

You've poisoned Europe, made it a cripple, and robbed it of its will to live. Yet we will bring Europe back to health. We will bring Europe freedom, real freedom. Freedom from you.

For we are generation identity.

27.

ON ETHNOPLURALISM

Since the dawn of history, humankind has been composed of innumerable cultures, peoples and tribes. Each has developed its own way of life, and an entirely unique way of seeing the world. The Native Americans strive for oneness with nature. The Japanese hold honour for their highest value; the drive toward freedom marks Europeans. Who would want to force all of these peoples and cultural milieus into one melting pot? Who would deny that they differ fundamentally, and that these differences are *good*?

Preserving cultural diversity and ensuring the most peaceful possible coexistence has always been our generation's great task. Deep in our hearts burns the desire to leave the era of hatred behind us. We want to visit other lands and peoples, get to know and love their unique characteristics, and avoid conflicts through better insight into the perspectives of other cultures.

Yet unlike you, we are no otherworldly fantasists about this. Peace among the peoples of the world is too important to be built on purely wishful thinking.

He who believes he can unite all cultures in multicultural societies doesn't do a service to peace, but lays the foundations for a future of war and hate.

*

Just as every person requires his own private place, every culture requires its own space in which to develop and structure everyday life according to its own manner.

He who drives all cultures and peoples together into one territory will cause the bloodiest wars, in the long term. Only by understanding this can the murderous Balkan Wars or the endless wars in the Middle East be explained.

Opposites placed in close proximity to one another always lead to conflict.

This rule also applies to Europe and the mass immigration of Muslims. History will show us once again that it would have been much more peaceful to send the immigrants home than to let them stay, and in so doing setting the stage for perpetual conflict.

*

But you've never understood the essence of identity and culture. You've never grasped that humans need space in order to live out their identities. That they absolutely want and require such a space, and will make it for themselves if given no other choice!

This is why the desires of countless peoples for their own territories has been causing tensions and clashes in Europe, and will one day again lead to bitter conflicts.

You will bear the guilt for these conflicts, not the combatants!

We, however, have understood the essence of identity and culture, and act in accordance with this understanding. Our politics won't be determined by illusions, but by the hard facts of reality. We respectfully acknowledge the longing for identity and every culture's right to its own space.

For we are generation identity.

28.

ON RESPONSIBILITY

Just as a doctor has a responsibility to his patients, a teacher to his students, a parent to his or her children, so we, generation identity, also have a responsibility to history.

That is to say, to those who come after us.

He who possesses or strives for power must always be held accountable for the responsible use of this power.

*

You wanted to escape this responsibility. You felt yourselves constrained. So you threw responsibility overboard, and with it all foresight, in order to experiment with Europe and the future of your children.

To whom do you truly owe answers?

You don't believe in God, your children don't figure into your calculations, and you don't care about Europe.

Yet you couldn't escape your historical responsibility. Consider the following: history is a merciless judge.

It will damn you for being those who drove Europe to the brink of total annihilation. It will remember that only the foresight and determination of your children tore Europe away from the abyss.

We, the identitarian generation, demand a future for Europe. And we will give Europe a future. Yet this future will demand of us lives of constant struggle. It will be torn by conflicts and battles that never would have been necessary if you had acted responsibly.

*

You ask how you have sinned? What were your crimes?

You've inflicted countless and terrible wounds on our planet. Wounds that we'll need to bandage and heal with the greatest care.

You've allowed an unprecedented demographic collapse, and so we'll need to cough up extravagant sums for your pensions. You've allowed, even promoted mass immigration, and so we'll need to fight for the right to own our continent one day.

This is the thread from which the battles and conflicts of the future are woven. This is the burden that you've passed down to us, your children.

We can only hope that this burden doesn't grow any bigger.

*

We are aware of our responsibility to history. We want to pass Europe on to our own children in a better state than we found it in. We want them to be able to live freely, without the worries that we have to bear.

To achieve this goal, we will relieve you of all your duties and all your power. Your politics is a dagger in our hearts, because it harms Europe.

For this reason, we strive for political and spiritual authority. We pursue politics of the grand style. But unlike you, we aren't afraid of assuming responsibility. We will take on both power and responsibility for the greater good of Europe.

For we are generation identity.

29.

ON THE GLOBALISED WORLD

We are truly living in a world that moves quickly. A world in which scientific discoveries multiply at breakneck pace, one technological revolution follows the next, and the world economy transforms itself beyond all recognition. What once lasted years and decades now takes place in days or hours.

We are entering a new era, an era of greater proximity and contact throughout the world. An era in which the great cultures clash with greater force than ever before in history. Peoples who once knew nothing of one another now encounter one another on a daily basis.

This is not always a good thing.

For globalisation is a double-edged sword.

It offers us previously unknown possibilities and opportunities. But even if controlled and properly managed, it still conceals previously unknown dangers.

*

Throughout most of human history, each culture lived in its own sphere without having much contact with the others.

In our more recent history, the cultures of the world lived under Western dominion.

That era, however, is drawing to a close. A plurality of cultures, each the worthy counterpart of the other, have stepped onto the world stage. Many of them possess powerful armies, powerful economies, and some of them have enough nuclear weapons to bring about a man-made apocalypse.

We must all be cautious in this new era. We can't afford to try to force our vision of the world on others out of vanity anymore.

The age clearly calls for consideration and respect for the identities of other cultures and religions. Above all, the West has a few lessons to learn in this regard.

*

But with the end of your power, Europe will also adapt. It will lay aside its arrogance and integrate itself into a new global society. This time, without prescriptions for how the rest of world ought to live.

This is our foreign policy.

In contrast to you, we've acknowledged the necessity for having consideration and respect for other cultures on their own terms, not the homogenisation of multiculturalism. Similarly, we've acknowledged the necessity for clear borders and geographic separation, in the interests of world peace.

*

Therefore we affirm the following:

China, live as you please, whether it is a dictatorship, a democracy, or a completely different form of government. It's not up to us to judge you. We will respect your noble culture, in any case.

Muslims, live as you please. Introduce Sharia, or perhaps not. You have the right to do whatever you consider to be right for your countries and in your culture. The time of 'liberation wars' has passed; let us be friends in the future.

To the Africans: the times in which we have robbed you of an independent voice must finally come to an end. We won't offer you any more hypocritical 'aid.' We won't try any longer to build your states according to our models. We will depart and let Africa be Africa. We will give you the chance to solve your problems yourselves, for you have the power to do so.

*

These are our vows of esteem and respect.

We request the following in return from other cultures:

Just as we accept your identity, we expect you to accept ours.

Recall your proselytisers. Stop forcing your way onto European territory. We all want to live together in a climate of mutual respect.

Our parents' era is over. The time in which Europe wanted to tell you how to live has come to an end. So has the time in which Europeans no longer cared about their own countries. In the epoch that is now beginning, the world may not be united, but it will certainly be marked by mutual respect.

This is the epoch of generation identity.

30.

ON ESCAPISM

The world, as it presents itself to us, is empty and cold. Its communities have been dissolved; what remains are individuals rushing madly to and fro in the service of the global economy.

It may not be surprising, therefore, that many of us escape into another, much more pleasant world — that of computer and video games.

There one finds that which no longer exists in the real world — a community to belong to, solidarity, great heroic deeds, authentic chivalry, and true love. In fact, video games are, for many of us, the last possibility to somehow perform heroic deeds, experience epic battles, achieve victory in combat, and overcome defeat.

This is why many of us choose this path, and some even forget their real lives in favour of it. They don't want to go back into the cold, senseless world that you've created, into which you've forced them.

You've nothing but disdain for their behaviour, and want to force them back into *your* reality. But they are fleeing from you.

We, however, understand our brothers and sisters. We know why they run, why they don't want to have anything more to do with this world, with *your* world.

So we say to you:

Come to us, brothers and sisters! In *this* life there are still battles to fight and struggles to win. We need your desire for action and your passion in order to defeat our parents.

Let's end their reign of terror together. Let's join each other in entering into a new era. Let's build a new world together. A world in which no one needs to run anymore. A world in which there will be genuine values and true friendship. A world of community and solidarity. Come to us, brothers and sisters. Join us in the struggle against the '68ers. Defend yourself with all your strength. Join us to reclaim our inheritance, our country, and our identity.

Come back, brothers and sisters! For we all belong together.

We are all generation identity.

31.

ON THE ZEITGEIST

Throughout Europe, your ideas and expectations form the dominant ideology. Laws were passed in accordance with your plans, and your neutered multicultural society became a reality. Your will became reality.

Yet how did it come to this? What is the basis for your power over Europe? Have you blackmailed and threatened the politicians? Have you all gone into politics yourselves? How were you able to so thoroughly implement your will?

The answer lies in the zeitgeist.

With your books and your art, your happenings and your music, you succeeded in shaping the zeitgeist of an entire generation. Surely only a few studied the complex theories that were the inspiration for it all, and yet you determined the social discourse, broke all the old taboos, and dominated all the dialogues.

It was not military superiority, nor economic power, nor the number of seats you had in the government, but rather your intellectual supremacy and dominance alone that brought you to power throughout Europe.

For this achievement you deserve our respect.

*

Still, you never managed to stabilise your power, and transmit your ideals to your children. Now a new generation is stepping up to the podium, a generation that decisively rejects your ideas. A generation that embodies its own, new zeitgeist. We are this generation. Step by step, we will challenge your intellectual superiority. We will write our own essays and books, sing our own songs, make videos, design graphics, create art, and daily weaken your grip on power in doing so.

There will come a day on which it is entirely natural for a student to be an identitarian, just as it was to be a Leftist in '68 and a Rightist in '33.

*

The battle with you will be difficult. You have powerful weapons at your command — TV broadcasters, newspapers, and political parties. In truth, your arsenal in this war appears to be limitless.

But in the end, we will take you down. Our will and our resolve will be put to many a difficult test, yet they will never yield. This is a battle for nothing less than our very selves. For Europe, our culture, and our identity!

We have thrown down the gauntlet.

For we are generation identity.

32.

ON THE LONGING FOR IDENTITY

Every human possesses not just one, but countless and diverse identities. Every one of us is a man or a woman, belongs to a nation, has a hometown, and is part of a religious community (or the community of the non-religious).

We possess countless identities, and only these make us who we are.

Yet you have declared war against them.

*

Identities are formed within a context of contrasts and boundaries. If there were no women, masculine identity would play no role for men. If Europe was alone in the world, the European identity would be meaningless. He who says 'Europe' must also say 'Asia' and 'Africa' in order to define its boundaries.

Every identity requires external boundaries. A young female solicitor will feel herself feminine among men, a lawyer among craftsmen, and young among older solicitors.

Identity requires distance. The inside requires an outside. The self needs an other. You have certainly acknowledged these laws. You blamed them for all the conflicts in the world.

This is why you launched your crusade against all identities. You still carry it on today with pitiless thoroughness.

*

You attacked the sexes with your neutered newspeak, gave dolls to boys, and robbed women of the enjoyment of their femininity.

You attacked religion by devaluing it and declaring it superfluous.

You attacked the world's cultures and nations by creating multicultural societies.

You attacked the notion of hometowns by trying to make all cities the same. Homogenisation and standardisation are truly the most powerful weapons in your struggle against identity.

For decades, you attacked all identities and tried to artificially overcome all your own contradictions. You fought this war savagely, with all means, and yet you have lost.

Your struggle against identity was in vain from the very beginning. The desire for one's own homeland, demarcated by borders, is stronger than everything else.

The will to identity is the greater power, one that not even you can fetter.

*

No matter how many dolls you dangle before the boys, they will always reach for the wooden swords. No matter how many laws and regulations you push through, there will always be male and female professions. The contrasts between cultures are nowhere more clearly visible than in your multicultural societies.

You can't defeat the will to identity.

Your campaign may have twisted and confused European identity, but it could never wipe it out. Your war leads to conflicts between the various types of identity, and yet their existence is just more evidence that you will never overcome identity.

*

Identity counts. Today, as in a thousand years.

We've given up fighting your senseless battles. We acknowledge that the wish for boundaries and the pursuit of identity are primal drives that will always be with us.

We won't waste any time fighting them — quite the opposite, as we hold them as being not only good, but necessary.

The will to identity is stronger than your artificial ideology. This is yet another reason that we will defeat you in the end. For we are generation identity.

33.

ON COMPULSORY MILITARY SERVICE

You were delayed only at one point during your march through the institutions. There was one organisation that you didn't bring under your control: the military.

Your character or psychology made you incapable or unwilling to join the military and to do there what you did in the universities, since you preferred the world of books to that of physical exertion and austerity.

Consequently, the military remains one of the last identitarian island strongholds in your sea of Leftist institutions.

Because you couldn't take over the military, you began to defame it. You dragged its name through the mud.

Soldiers can only be led with discipline, obedience, and camaraderie. An anti-authoritarian army is unthinkable, therefore every military organisation is the natural enemy of your ideology.

So it came to pass that the young men you raised to be feminine and question authority landed in the barracks of the European armies, where they made up in months of training what your society had neglected for years. The armies drilled the youth and accomplished an indispensable educational mission in doing so.

If there is still any masculinity, honour, and camaraderie today, the credit is due, above all, to the hard training that men received in the barracks.

*

This training was a thorn in your side. So you attacked compulsory military service and tried to abolish it. Not for military reasons, but because obedience and drills didn't fit into your worldview.

When the Soviet Union finally imploded, you immediately set yourselves to the task of eliminating the draft. It was never about reforming the military; it was always intended to serve your ideological goals.

By abolishing the draft in many countries, and attempting to do so in countless more, you've done incalculable damage to our societies.

You robbed our generation of the last chance to prove itself. You stole this chance for us to get to know our limits. How happy those of us are who still had this chance!

Many of us haven't a clue how strong we truly are, nor what we can achieve or withstand.

We want to find out. We want to push our own limits. Unlike you, we want to know ourselves.

We are not afraid to obey. We are not afraid to fight, and if need be, to make the ultimate sacrifice. We know that a man needs to be able to take the shouting of the drill sergeant—only boys and weaklings 'discuss.' Men accept or act. The army once taught this.

*

From a military perspective, compulsory service in Europe may or may not be necessary. Yet it is certainly necessary from a societal perspective.

We affirm the clear virtues of this, the greatest of educators of the youth. We were and always will be in favour of compulsory military service, for our country and its civil solidarity.

For we are generation identity.

34.

ON INTEGRATION

One day you recognised that your multicultural society faced rejection among the peoples of Europe, that Europeans don't want it. Countless lands raised their voices in cries of protest, and Right-wing parties won votes. You had to react.

So you presented our ailing continent with another magical cure: integration.

You acted as if integration were something new, as if it were the opposite of multiculturalism. In this way you sought to placate the peoples of Europe, at least until the foreign communities were strong enough in our lands to put a stop to all protests against the multicultural society.

So it was that you pulled the wool over the eyes of the European peoples.

*

There are two definitions of integration. You always used the one you found suited to your particular audience of the moment. When you talked to the immigrants, you demanded that they work and master the language of the land. But how do a job and language skills change the fact of a multicultural society?

When you talked to the Europeans, you used an entirely different definition of integration. You spoke of Western values and said that eventually one would no longer be able to differentiate the migrants from ethnic Europeans, that they would become culturally identical. You essentially said that, with time, they would assume a European identity.

With these words you sought to placate the Europeans. That worked for a while.

But at some point, the Right-wing parties caught on to your trick and finally demanded a 'harder' integration. That is to say, what you had promised the Europeans.

But even this demand is deceptive.

What reason would the members of increasingly powerful communities have to join a decadent and dying European culture? How can true integration be possible when non-Europeans are already so numerous that they can live effortlessly in their parallel societies?

*

We reject this fake confrontation between you and the populist Right-wing parties. We neither want a multicultural society, nor do we want to force members of other cultures to take on our identity. We therefore affirm the following:

'68ers! Stop preaching a social model that can't work, and immediately plunges societies into chaos whenever it is attempted.

Right-wingers! Stop defaming immigrants, stop insulting them and blaming them for our mistakes.

Stop accusing them for wanting to hold on to their identities. There is nothing crueller than to demand that one give up his very self.

Muslims and Africans! Take down your tents and leave this continent. Entire regions of the world already belong to you. We'll gladly help you make your homelands better places, help you to build and shape them. Even more so than European help, Africa and the global East need you and your strength.

Return to your home countries, for they belong to you.

Europe, however, will never belong to you. Europe belongs to us.

For we are generation identity.

35.

ON A WORLD WITHOUT IDENTITIES

Let's imagine for a moment that your vision of a world without oppositions, in other words, a world without differences, was realisable. Let's picture for just a moment how such a world would look. Then you'll understand, as far as is possible, why we will never share your goals. Why we will and must always fight you. Let's scout the terrain into which your ideology will lead us in the end.

*

Your world is grey. There are no more colours. Aren't colours the reason for conflicts, hate, and war? Didn't whites always fight against blacks, reds against yellows?

Therefore you've abolished colours, for they only divide and lead to fascistic groupthink.

Trekking through your world, we reach a city. A city in which all the streets and buildings look precisely the same. Don't different buildings necessarily lead to envy and social strife? Doesn't everyone want to show off and show his superiority with the appearance of his home?

So you tore down all the old houses and built new, completely identical ones. It is forbidden under penalty of law to alter one's home in any way.

The people in your world, men and women alike, all wear the same clothing. Different clothing also leads to exclusion and groupthink.

We enter one of your many education factories. Here infants, taken from their parents shortly after birth, are raised by highly trained and qualified experts. You've recognised that many people are disadvantaged by their family backgrounds. To give everyone the same chances in life, you've finally abolished the outmoded institution of the family.

The children are taught some things in school. But they don't receive grades, because grades differentiate the better from the less capable students.

No one is forced to pay attention in class, and those who do are regularly punished, because they make their peers look inferior.

We leave the factory and head towards the city centre. Where once a cathedral stood, today there is only a massive crater in the ground. Since you have recognised that religions were the cause of countless wars, you burned all churches, shrines, mosques, temples, and monasteries to the ground. These establishments harboured differences.

We talk to a passer-by, but he can't understand us. He cannot even speak. You've recognised that all forms of language divide the world. And is not that the first step to mass murder and war?

*

So we wander through your ever-so-peaceful world, a world in which there are no more wars, no more conflicts, and no more struggles.

To what end would one still fight wars here? How could a conflict of any kind arise in such a place? What would one fight for in this world of yours, where there's nothing worth the effort?

Your dream is our nightmare.

For we are generation identity.

36.

ON THE CONFLICT IN THE MIDDLE EAST

Yes, we also want to discuss this most explosive of issues, for nowhere does the unrealistic character of your ideology and the failure of your politics become more clear than when it concerns Israel and Palestine.

Here your complete helplessness in the face of the brutal struggles of the real world is on display.

In the deserts of the holy land, the ancient traditions of two peoples collide, and they both fight for their highest values, the holy sites of their national, cultural, and religious identities.

*

You've never understood this conflict. You've always organised ceasefire talks, peace processes, and meetings of all sorts, but you were disappointed again and again.

The failure of all your efforts was completely predictable, at least for those who understood the causes of the conflict.

This conflict is neither of an economic nor a political nature; it is entirely cultural. This struggle isn't about money or resources, but symbols and holy places.

The Israelis and the Palestinians don't both claim the Temple Mount because it brings them copious revenue, but because it forms the centre of their respective identities.

Neither side can or ever will give up the Temple Mount or drop their claim to it, for it symbolises what they consider to be their holy lands.

There is no solution and no peace in this war, and that you still believe in peace after more than 60 years of war only shows how incorrigible you are.

Peace can't be achieved with feeble appeals, but only by neutralising the driving force of the conflict.

The driving force of this conflict is the identity of both peoples. As long as there are both Palestinians and Israelis in the holy land, these two peoples will stand at odds.

*

While Israelis and Palestinians fight for their homeland, we watch with utter disgust as you interfere in the conflict and take sides.

You tend to try and identify the good and evil sides in every conflict, but we believe in neither the one nor the other in this case.

Whichever side you pick, we reject your partisanship.

Who would fault the Jews for wanting to return to their homeland after millennia of persecution and homelessness? Who would fault the Palestinians for wanting to remain in their homeland?

*

Wars, conflicts, and hate that persist for decades are the result when different peoples are forced to be together in the same territory. Thanks to you, a similar fate threatens Europe.

In the war for the Middle East, however, we remain neutral. Neither party is good or evil. Both peoples must fight, because they can't do otherwise. We understand this and hope that Europe is spared similar conflicts. We struggle for peace.

For we are generation identity.

37.

ON ART

As everyone knows, there is no accounting for taste and every attempt at defining a definitive aesthetic standard is inherently impossible.

We aren't so arrogant as to claim to be able to define what is beautiful and what is not, just as we will not claim to stand on the side of 'true' or 'real' art.

In any case, beauty may be relative, but what a person or culture finds beautiful says a great deal about that person or culture.

*

In ancient times, the Roman principle applied—art should portray the world more beautifully than it actually appears. This principle was an expression of the Roman character, of a longing for that which is higher, the eternal.

The Romans constructed monumental structures, marble statues and magnificent temples. They were perfect in form, radiating strength and transcendence.

A culture's art has always been an expression of the quality of its lived experience. Great empires erected gigantic structures. Freedom-loving peoples wrote dramas and poems in praise of freedom and love.

*

But what did you create? Formless, meaningless, unprecedented, 'modern' works. Your art betrays everything about you.

You lacked all will to form, all will to creation. Your minds are swamps of chaos, constant conflict, and self-hate.

Accordingly, you create fractured and shattered works of art, reflecting the full extent of your spiritual suffering.

One can't argue about taste. If you find such things beautiful, then so be it. But let it be said:

We don't find it beautiful! Our stomachs turn at the thought of your modern art. Your attempts to be 'original' are our eyesores.

Kindly spare us the visits to your galleries, and never force us to look at the like of them again.

Even if there were no political reasons to remove you from power, your artwork would be quite enough.

We love a different kind of art—the sort that stands in unity with the natural world, the sort that radiates pride and glory, that represents something real and in which we can find meaning. Not chaos, but order. Not a monotonous mixture, but the glimmering purity of all the colours.

That is what we find beautiful.

For we are generation identity.

38.

AUREA AETAS: THE GOLDEN ERA

Whoever is genuinely familiar with the Mayan prophecies knows that they predicted that 21 December 2012 would mark not the end of the world, but the beginning of a new era.

A new global era that would be fundamentally different from the one that came before it.

Whether or not one believes in mystical scriptures, it is nonetheless in our power to bring about such a new era. A golden era of identity.

*

We want to create a new world. We want to rebuild our planet upon a new foundation, and abandon the path that we are on, which leads to the faceless and homogenised average man.

We want to reawaken the tumult of the storm, the inconceivable pattern of all things. Our new era shall not ripple forward mildly like a tamed river, monotonous and always the same.

Quite the opposite! Smash the dams, brothers and sisters! This era shall be a wild and unvanquished riptide! Its every bend, every strait, and every waterfall are to be unique.

*

Smash your chains, brother and sisters! The '68ers have penned us up, to make us all alike. But we love difference! Rip down the artificial walls of our common prison! Be men and women, Europeans and Asians again!

*

Defend nature, dear siblings!

Every tree, every stone, and every mountain is sacred to us. We won't allow our country's beauty to be measured by its economic value any longer!

*

Lay aside your animosity, peoples of the world! Let's stop trying to create a united world by dominating others. Let's not attempt to force our cultures and religions on one another any longer. Instead, let's preserve our own identities and *truly* learn to love diversity!

*

Let's reign in the economy, and stop being the slaves of the tiny elite of the wealthy! We'll free our planet from the deathly grip of capitalism and create a society in which the economy serves culture, and not the reverse.

Brothers and sisters: the golden era begins within and with us. It is in our hands to create a new and better world.

We will demolish the dungeons of the '68ers, and this era will become reality.

*

Dear brothers and sisters!

Our identity lies in chains, confined and tortured, oppressed and raped, abused and despairing. It had to suffer countless monstrosities and indignities without number.

Let's end the suffering. This is our liberation song.

39.

OUR DECISION

Brothers and sisters!

We know how you feel at this moment. Your feelings are ours. The same doubt, the same uncertainty tears at us all.

*

History has put before us the greatest imaginable test. We grew up upon a continent that has long forgotten itself. We were raised by parents who were determined to destroy our countries while being surrounded by vital and strong foreign peoples who are striving for the riches of an enfeebled Europe.

This is our fate. A fate that we cannot escape. Whether we want it or not, whether we recognise it or not, whether we accept it or deny it, it is and remains our fate.

And yet we have a choice. Each one of must make a decision for himself.

Each of us must decide. Do we want to tackle the challenge that history presents to us together, or do we want to give up and let Europe fall?

It is a difficult decision, and no one should make it lightly. Every choice brings heavy consequences.

*

If we let Europe die, we can still retreat. We can leave the political sphere, give up the big cities, and migrate with our families to remote villages. We can still lead a happy life in peace, quiet, and seclusion. We can flee from all the decadence of our society, for there are still other places where we can take refuge. Nothing stops us from achieving personal happiness.

But if we do this, if we give up and retreat, then Europe will undeniably and permanently decline and fall.

Isn't that fine, so long as we can still live our own lives happily and peacefully?

*

We might also come to a different conclusion. We could proudly and bravely declare, 'Europe will never pass away! We will never let Europe die!'

If we were to say this, if enough of us were to say it, if enough of us would stand up and fight, if we can find the courage for this decision, then yes, Europe will live. Then this continent will be born again, and enter a new era of freedom. We will be the heroes of future history.

*

This decision will mean a great deal of personal suffering.

It means a fight. Not for weeks or months, but for years and decades, a fight that will tax and take its toll upon each of us.

It means standing up. Standing up against our parents, against the state, against politics, against all who claim to be able to determine our future for us.

It means raising our voices, speaking out when our identity is defamed, interrupting when everyone else is in passive agreement.

It means dispute. It means passionate discussion, without ever doubting the justice of our cause.

It means conflict. Conflict with our families, our teachers and professors, and with all whose respect we would actually prefer to win.

*

Think hard about this decision. Once you make it, you can never take it back. Once you've chosen the struggle for our identity, it will never again leave you in peace. You can never retreat, for you'll never be happy until our country is saved.

Brothers and sisters, this is our fate, our decision.

For we are generation identity.

40.

OUR WEAPONS

Brothers and sisters!

Our struggle is hard and our opponents know no mercy. They hate us for robbing them of their illusions.

Know that they will use every trick and ruse at their disposal.

They will abuse us in the media, ignore and humiliate us, and do everything but talk to us.

Don't expect an open dialogue or a lively exchange of arguments. Don't expect them to obey the rules. They won't, and so neither can we.

There will only be a dialogue if we force them into one. Therefore we must seek out confrontation. We have to yell and scream so loudly that no one can ignore us any longer. To this end, we need a courageous and innovative movement.

A movement that acts instead of waits. It needs action instead of reaction, passion instead of cold detachment, bravery instead of cowardice, mental agility and flexibility instead of paralysis and conservatism, love instead of hate, community instead of individualism.

A movement such as has seldom been seen before, and will seldom be seen again.

*

We need to throw all of our ballast overboard in order to stay buoyant. We are at war with enemies who enjoy an enormous advantage.

They control an arsenal of weapons we can't even dream of—newspapers, TV stations, political parties, and governments. They dominate the public discourse, and conspire with one another.

If we want to win this struggle, we need to armour up.

We must forge intellectual weapons, for our armouries are empty.

Write books, brothers and sisters, for every sentence ignites passion in a thousand others.

Sing songs, brothers and sisters, for a song can move the entire world.

Draw pictures and make videos, for these say more than words ever could.

We need every weapon we can lay our hands on. Every one of you has a talent you can use in the fight. Help us forge the weapons we will wield in battle against the '68ers. We will defeat them.

For we are generation identity.

41.

THE DECLARATION OF WAR

'68ers!

We've laid out our arguments in their entirety. At last!

We've analysed your deeds and your influence in a wide array of settings. We know what you wanted and what you realised.

We grasp you and your doings even better than yourselves. Now hear our verdict:

Now and for all times, we declare you to be the downfall and undoing of Europe and the world. You are the enemies of all identities and the opponents of all forms of diversity.

You abhor everything vibrant and colourful. You knowingly destroyed everything that was holy to us and to our ancestors. You damned us to this life in a pale twilight. You murdered our siblings and abandoned your responsibilities.

You fought against everything natural and killed everything that had grown up over centuries. Now we are bringing you to justice.

We will tear the sceptre of power from your trembling hands. If you don't want to give it up, we will fight you until you're dethroned and rendered harmless.

However long it may take, whatever it may cost, we will defeat you. Your era is at an end. We'll sweep your delusional ideas out along with you. You should know that we will eradicate the power structures you used to dominate us, root and branch.

*

Our patience has reached its end.

Don't think of this book as a manifesto. It's a declaration of war. Our war against you.

Other books published by Arktos:

Beyond Human Rights
by Alain de Benoist

Manifesto for a European Renaissance
by Alain de Benoist & Charles Champetier

The Problem of Democracy
by Alain de Benoist

Germany's Third Empire
by Arthur Moeller van den Bruck

The Arctic Home in the Vedas
by Bal Gangadhar Tilak

Revolution from Above
by Kerry Bolton

The Fourth Political Theory
by Alexander Dugin

Fascism Viewed from the Right
by Julius Evola

Metaphysics of War
by Julius Evola

The Path of Cinnabar
by Julius Evola

Archeofuturism
by Guillaume Faye

Convergence of Catastrophes
by Guillaume Faye

Why We Fight
by Guillaume Faye

The WASP Question
by Andrew Fraser

War and Democracy
by Paul Gottfried

The Saga of the Aryan Race
by Porus Homi Havewala

Homo Maximus
by Lars Holger Holm

The Owls of Afrasiab
by Lars Holger Holm

De Naturae Natura
by Alexander Jacob

Fighting for the Essence
by Pierre Krebs

Can Life Prevail?
by Pentti Linkola

Guillaume Faye and the Battle of Europe
by Michael O'Meara

The Ten Commandments of Propaganda
by Brian Anse Patrick

A Handbook of Traditional Living
by Raido

The Agni and the Ecstasy
by Steven J. Rosen

The Jedi in the Lotus
by Steven J. Rosen

It Cannot Be Stormed
by Ernst von Salomon

Tradition & Revolution
by Troy Southgate

Against Democracy and Equality
by Tomislav Sunic

The Initiate: Journal of Traditional Studies
by David J. Wingfield (ed.)